MEET THE KNIGHTS

Written by Julia March

Editor Pamela Afram
Project Art Editor Jon Hall
Designer Jade Wheaton
Pre-Production Producer Siu Yin Chan
Producer Louise Daly
Managing Editor Paula Regan
Managing Art Editor Guy Harvey
Art Director Lisa Lanzarini
Publisher Julie Ferris
Publishing Director Simon Beecroft

Reading Consultant
Maureen Fernandes

First published in Great Britain in 2016 by
Dorling Kindersley Limited
80 Strand, London WC2R 0RL
A Penguin Random House Company

10 9 8 7 6 5 4 3 2 1
001–288030–March/2016

Page design copyright © 2016
Dorling Kindersley Limited

A CIP catalogue record for this book
is available from the British Library.

ISBN: 978-0-24123-708-3

Printed and bound in China

www.LEGO.com
www.dk.com

A WORLD OF IDEAS:
SEE ALL THERE IS TO KNOW

LEGO® NEXO KNIGHTS™: MERLOK 2.0

Free app • Kostenlose App • Appli gratuite
App gratis • App Grátis • Ingyenes alkalmazás

Device check: Gerät prüfen: Vérification du dispositif:
Comprueba tu dispositivo: Verificação do dispositivo:
Eszközellenőrzés: **LEGO.COM/devicecheck**

Each of the knights has a Shield Power
you can scan. Here is Axl's:

There are four other scannable shields within
the pages of this book – can you find them?

Contents

Welcome to Knighton

The land of Knighton is a mix of old and new. Knights wear high-tech armour and play computer games. Castles stand side by side with cinemas and shopping centres. The kingdom is ruled by King and Queen Halbert.

GRADUATION DAY

Five young pages have graduated from The Knights' Academy. All the knights are very different. Each one has promised to protect Knighton from danger.

CLAY

"A great knight follows the Knights' Code."

LANCE

"This could make me a star..."

MACY

"I can be a princess and a knight!"

AARON

"This could be dangerous. Cool!"

AXL

"Do they serve snacks in a battle?"

Clay

Clay wants to be the best knight ever. He trains for hours and hours every day. He has learnt the Knights' Code by heart, too. No wonder Clay was top of the class at The Knights' Academy.

Lance

Lance is a bit of a show-off.
He loves to look good. Lance
makes sure his armour is extra
shiny. He spends lots of money
on armour polish. Good job
he is super rich!

Macy

Macy is a princess. She does not like it! Life in the castle is so boring. It is all sparkly dresses and silly dances. Macy cannot wait to be a knight and have adventures.

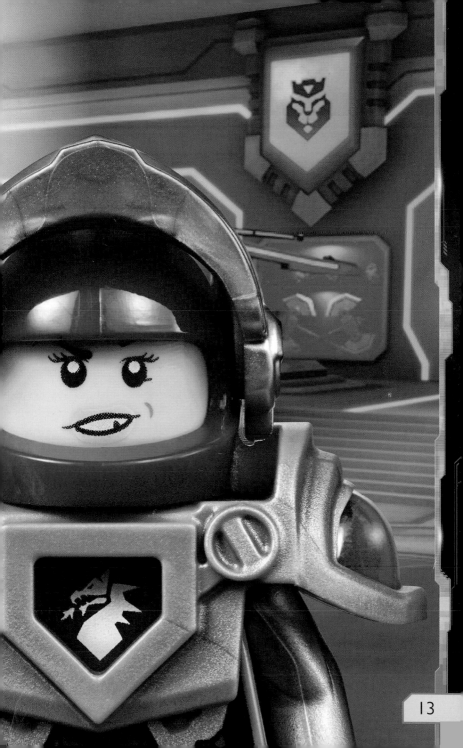

Queen Halbert's Email

From: Macy Halbert

Dear Mum,

I just wanted you to know that I am doing great! Now that I am a real knight, I am helping to protect Knighton. I hope Dad will see how good I am at being a knight, too.

We are looking forward to coming to the castle for a big feast. Especially Axl!

Lots of love,

Princess Macy

1 Attachment 📎

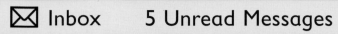 Inbox   5 Unread Messages
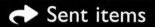 Sent items
 Trash
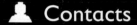 Contacts
 Folders

This is me fighting the Beast Master!

Aaron

Aaron is a thrill-seeker. He loves crazy games and sports. So what if there is a chance things could go wrong? That makes it all the more fun!

Axl

Axl loves to eat. He also loves playing with his band, the Boogie Knights. Axl's favourite song goes like this:

"Oh I am a knight
Who likes a bite
So give me steak,
And beans, and cake!"

Jestro

Jestro is King Halbert's jester.
He does not like being a jester
because people say he is not
very good at it.

Jestro finds some books of dark magic. The king's wizard casts a spell to stop him from using them. KA-BOOM! Jestro and the books are thrown across Knighton.

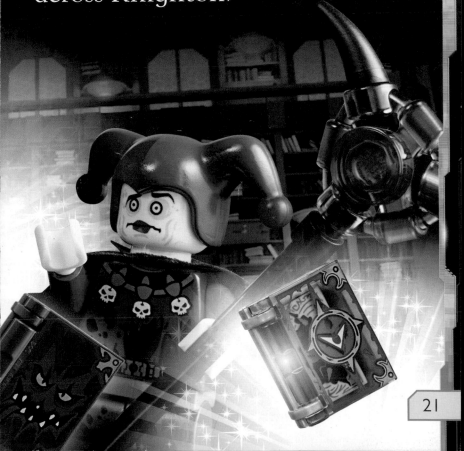

A BLOW FOR JESTRO

The joke really was on Jestro.

NEWS

Hundreds of people came to watch
King Halbert's jester, Jestro, perform
last night. Jestro's act got plenty
of laughs – but only because it all
went wrong. Oh dear!
Jestro forgot his jokes. He tripped
over his feet. He tried to juggle,
but dropped the balls. The jester
even caused a power cut in Knighton.
Poor Jestro. What a failure!

The Book of Monsters

Jestro finds the Book of Monsters. The book wants to scare people. But first, it needs help to free the monsters trapped inside it.

Jestro is angry at everyone
who laughed at him. He will
help the Book of Monsters
scare people!

WARNING!

MAGMA MONSTERS

Monsters have been spotted in the kingdom. Watch out for their fiery weapons and blazing tempers. Citizens of Knighton beware! If you see a Magma Monster... RUN!

HOT-HEADED
SPARKKS

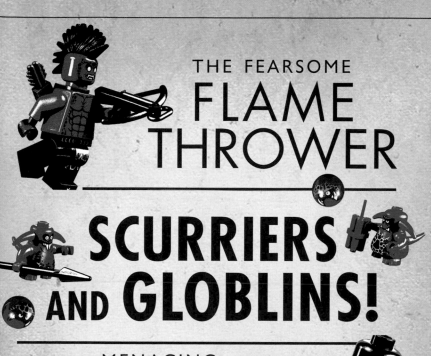

THE FEARSOME
FLAME THROWER

SCURRIERS
AND GLOBLINS!

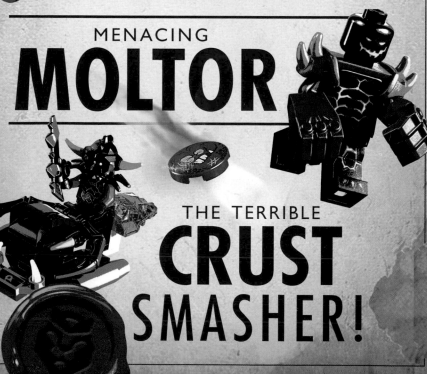

MENACING
MOLTOR

THE TERRIBLE
CRUST SMASHER!

Ava and Merlok 2.0

Ava Prentiss is a very clever
student at the Knights' Academy.
She finds out that the king's
wizard, Merlok, has been sucked
into the castle's computer system.
Now he is Merlok 2.0.
Merlok 2.0 will be able to help
the knights protect Knighton!

The Fortrex

Jestro and his monsters
are causing havoc all over
Knighton. The knights must
stop them. They pile their
gear into a rolling castle
called The Fortrex. Merlok
2.0 can come as well.
Hurry up, knights!

INSIDE
THE FORTREX

Royal banner hologram

Prison

Rapid fire shooter

Tank treads

The Fortrex is like a castle on tank treads. It has a training area for the knights to practise their skills. Merlok 2.0 is part of The Fortrex computer system. He can send powers to the knights' special shields.

Wi-Fi antenna

Control room

Plasma guns

Drawbridge

NEXO Powers

Merlok 2.0 uploads digital powers to the knights. They are called NEXO Powers. NEXO Powers give the knights special monster-fighting abilities. Their weapons glow bright orange, too. Now they are ready for battle!

"NEXO Powers are great! Clapper Claw allows me to swing my mace with dragon strength!

POWERS DO?

"Merlok 2.0 sent
Toxic Sting power to my
NEXO Shield. It creates
a cloud of deadly gas.
Watch out monsters!"

Knights vs Monsters

The monsters fire their Chaos Catapult at the NEXO KNIGHTS™ heroes. Ouch! But the knights have their own vehicles.

Here comes Clay, driving his Rumble Blade. The monsters do not like the look of that big sword at the front!

Jestro Defeated

The monsters keep attacking Knighton. You can beat them, brave knights!

The knights finally chase off Jestro and his monsters. The King and Queen are so happy. The knights have saved the kingdom.

Quiz

1. Who rules Knighton?

2. Which knight loves crazy games and sports?

3. Why does Macy not like life in the castle?

4. What is the name of King Halbert's jester?

5. What colour do NEXO weapons glow?

6. What is the name of the knights' rolling castle?

7. Which knight loves to eat?

8. Who uploads NEXO Powers to the knights?

9. Who drives the Rumble Blade?

10. Which knight keeps his armour extra shiny?

Answers on page 45

Glossary

Academy
A school where people can learn special skills.

Graduate
To successfully complete a course of study.

Havoc
Damage and confusion.

Jester
A servant of a king or queen whose job is to make people laugh.

Mace
A heavy club used as a weapon.

Magma
Melted rock from under the Earth's surface.

Page
Someone who is training to be a knight.

Index

Answers to the quiz on pages 42 and 43:
1. King and Queen Halbert 2. Aaron 3. It is so boring!
4. Jestro 5. Orange 6. The Fortrex 7. Axl 8. Merlok 2.0
9. Clay 10. Lance
Scannable shields can be found on pages 2, 4, 14, 36 and 44.

Guide for Parents

DK Reads is a three-level reading series for children, developing the habit of reading widely for both pleasure and information. These books have exciting running text interspersed with a range of reading genres to suit your child's reading ability, as required by the school curriculum. Each book is designed to develop your child's reading skills, fluency, grammar awareness and comprehension in order to build confidence and engagement when reading.

Ready for a *Beginning to Read* book
YOUR CHILD SHOULD

- be using phonics, including combinations of consonants, such as bl, gl and sm, to read unfamiliar words; and common word endings, such as plurals, ing, ed and ly.

- be using the storyline, illustrations and the grammar of a sentence to check and correct their own reading.

- be pausing briefly at commas, and for longer at full stops; and altering his/her expression to respond to question, exclamation and speech marks.

A Valuable And Shared Reading Experience

For many children, reading requires much effort but adult participation can make this both fun and easier. So here are a few tips on how to use this book with your child.

TIP 1: Check out the contents together before your child begins:

- Read the text about the book on the back cover.

- Read through and discuss the contents page together to heighten your child's interest and expectation.

- Briefly discuss any unfamiliar or difficult words on the contents page.

- Chat about the non-fiction reading features used in the book, such as headings, captions, recipes, lists or charts.

This introduction helps to put your child in control and makes the reading challenge less daunting.

TIP 2: Support your child as he/she reads the story pages:

- Give the book to your child to read and turn the pages.

- Where necessary, encourage your child to break a word into syllables, sound out each one and then flow the syllables together. Ask him/her to reread the sentence to check the meaning.

- When there's a question mark or an exclamation mark, encourage your child to vary his/her voice as he/she reads the sentence. Demonstrate how to do this if it is helpful.

TIP 3: Praise, share and chat:

- The factual pages tend to be more difficult than the story pages, and are designed to be shared with your child.

- Ask questions about the text and the meaning of the words used. Ask your child to suggest his/her own quiz questions. These help to develop comprehension skills and awareness of the language used.

A FEW ADDITIONAL TIPS

- Try and read together every day. Little and often is best. After 10 minutes, only keep going if your child wants to read on.

- Always encourage your child to have a go at reading difficult words by themselves. Praise any self-corrections, for example, "I like the way you sounded out that word and then changed the way you said it, to make sense."

- Read other books of different types to your child just for enjoyment and information.

Have you read these other great books from DK?

BEGINNING TO READ

Find out what happens on a farm through the seasons.

Discover how the bravest Ninja in the land save Ninjago.

Meet a host of rebels as they fight for freedom from the Empire.

STARTING TO READ ALONE

Travel through the asteroid belt to the king of the planets – Jupiter.

Discover the new tribes threatening Chima™ with their icy powers.

Buckle up and get ready for an action-packed ride!